R0082992710

03/2015

Don't Trip, Pip!

by Marie Powell

illustrated by Amy Cartwright

Ideas for Parents and Teachers

Amicus Readers let children practice reading at early reading levels. Familiar words and concepts with close illustration-text matches support early readers.

Before Reading
- Discuss the cover illustration with the child. What does it tell him?
- Ask the child to predict what she will learn in the book.

Read the Book
- "Walk" through the book and look at the illustrations. Let the child ask questions.
- Point out the colored words. Ask the child what is the same about them (spelling, ending sound).
- Read the book to the child, or have the child read to you.

After Reading
- Use the word family list at the end of the book to review the text.
- Prompt the child to make connections. Ask: *What other words end with -ip?*

Amicus Readers are published by Amicus
P.O. Box 1329, Mankato, MN 56002
www.amicuspublishing.us

Illustrations by Amy Cartwright

Produced for Amicus by The Peterson Publishing Company and Red Line Editorial.

Editor Jenna Gleisner
Designer Craig Hinton
Printed in the United States of America
Mankato, MN
1-2014
PA10001
10 9 8 7 6 5 4 3 2 1

Library of Congress Cataloging-in-Publication Data
Powell, Marie, 1958-
  Don't trip, pip! / Marie Powell.
     pages cm. -- (Word families)
  Audience: Age 6.
  K to Grade 3.
   ISBN 978-1-60753-580-5 (hardcover) --
   ISBN 978-1-60753-646-8 (pdf ebook)
  1. Reading--Phonetic method. 2. Readers (Primary) I. Title.
   LB1573.3.P6934 2014
   372.46'5--dc23
                              2013043997

My name is **Kip**. This is my dog, **Pip**.

I teach Pip tricks. But Pip always seems to trip!

I flip a toy into the air. "Catch it, Pip!" I say. He leaps up. But his feet trip on the rug.

The lamp starts to **tip**.

I run to catch it.

Pip wags his tail. He is okay.

"Time for a drink, Pip,"
I say. He laps up his water.
He does not sip.
I say, "Slow down or you
will drip!"

PIP

I **grip** a treat in my hand and say, "Sit."
Pip sits with his paws up. His back legs **slip**. He yelps, "**Yip!**"

We try our tricks outside.
Pip's front feet skip over
a branch.
I say, "Look out! Don't
trip, Pip!"

Word Family: -ip

Word families are groups of words that rhyme and are spelled the same.

Here are the -ip words in this book:

drip	skip
flip	slip
grip	tip
Kip	trip
Pip	yip
sip	

Can you spell any other words with -ip?